Farewell Dundrennan

Farewell Dundrennan

Len Irving

drawings by
Elinor Randall

The Stone Circle Press

Library of Congress Catalogue Number 87-061208

ISBN 0-9618699-0-9

Published by Stone Circle Press
Box 44, Oakland, California, 94604.

Tae the Auld Wa's

Grateful acknowledgement to the following publications in which two of these poems appeared: April Again, in the *DeKalb Literary Arts Journal*, and The Big Beast is Back in *The Burning World.*

The author wishes to express his gratitude to the Institute of Celtic Studies for making this publication possible, with financial, technical and social aid.

Contents

Farewell Dundrennan

The cottage was a haven for phantoms.
Dragon movements coiled
inside the casters of the bed
and the quilt was a restless fox.
On nights when the wind blew
the windows inside out
the floral wallpaper
became a breeding ground
for arthritic spiders
playing leapfrog with bunnies
whose faces resembled Grecian urns.
And outside, trolls piss fell
heavier than rain.
Bewildered sheep in black fleeces
bleated as I counted the stars I saw
through the bedroom ceiling,
and farther away than downstairs,
Father listened to an ancient wireless set
that, with cracks of lightning,
sounded lonelier
than any somber sea.

Birthplace

Now the yew trees are again still.
The lute of time plays
Across the Solway Firth.
Gladiolas breathe faintly on Fagara Hill.
Behind an abandoned garden
Where all but the wind is restless,
Windowless and deserted,
The cottage where I was born
Falls apart.

Ghost-Drawn

Ghost-drawn and swan-feathered
dropped from space
wafted on silent wings
to where deep voices
mourn over a burial ground
of lost bards
lying cat-light
wailing a keen
for language lost.
Once fine-fingered and warmed by sunlight
sang and lyred their instruments
with hands now turned to stone.
Only cold stars remained
longer than light
deeper than need
farther than lost desire
empty as always
before time and distance
squandered our footpath to the sun.
Oh we were young then
and blazed through sky
our moon-white way.
Blind men
leading cripples
into terrible and impenetrable thickets.
Ghost-drawn and swan-driven
Where did our destination lead ?
Where ? Tell me where ?
And what our purpose ?

The Phantom Deer of Inverness

The phantom deer of Inverness
brushing shoulders or sidling alone,
trackless - untraceable,
leading one to wonder
do they even exist ?
Silently gliding,
farther than the edge of eyesight,
the shadows of their shadows
move beyond shades of being,
presenting not themselves,
but visions of themselves,
white and ghostly,
to only some few,
and even then most rarely,
no more to be accurately described
than recognition
of footprints
fading
on a smooth pond's surface.

Shadows Like Horses

Down palisades of night
bunched or racing in death-seeking gallop
see the darkening cloud as their shadows
break the starting gate
hear the faint small-rumbling
vibrations of charging hooves.
Single arrogant stallion-shapes,
piebald mares, tough as barbed wire,
shrieking hysterically
attempting abandon their phantasmal selves
break through into another reality.

I Saw a Horse

From this cathouse of dreams
I saw a horse
with hooves of steel
huge-chested
straining withers
foam on his tongue.
In those fire-fly eyes
a courtesan's image danced.

In the course of his passing
trees melted into candles
startled trout sprang from their pools
bogs and marshes boiled.
Pausing by riverside in strange moonlight
the ins and outs of his breath
seemed to resemble
all the terrors
of making love.

Preoccupation

Down brows of lost countries
the green hills remain.
Through orchards of lost cradles
Spring continues to rule.
New growth of heavy pasture
rises to the sun.

But here
in the decayed hills
the yellow cargo of apples
we once held to our breasts
and cider
sharp as knives
to slake our thirsts
are wrinkled now.

Beyond scope of memory
and too slow for human vision
a rake of wind
gnaws the mountain away.

Superstitions

Every other leap year
walking under ladders
my wishbone blood erupts.
Down hallways of cracked mirrors
cloverleafs await my plucking.
She loves me.
She loves me not.
She loves me.
Cheers.
I'll drink to that.
Beneath the sign of the ram
I'll sing thirteen songs
seven time seven times over.
Good looking women will fall
to my rabbit-footed blarney
under the full
of the mistletoe-kissing room.

The Blue Iris

Outdoors
the blue iris
a butterfly of flowers
wind-swayed for take-off
is poised
unable to rise
tied to earth
by her terrible roots.

Indoors
stem severed
this flowering butterfly
free now from earth
poised still
maiden flight untaken
permits her head to droop.

Preface to a Hangover

When the slanting
picture-rail horizon
adjusts to its true level
and the light fixture
re-attaches itself
to the floating light-bulb;
when the tail
of a flame-throated
alligator
returns inside his
ceiling crevice
I know morning is near
and everything in the house
long drunk up.

The Big Beast is Back

Loose lips babbling
in a squabble
of rabble-rousing language
as a musk-reeking turkey
totters all about
before joining me
to slurp cheap vodka
from a bottle
all but emptied now.
Slice the situation
any way you will,
we still know it is
too late.
Padlock the cell door
the good grey mare
is again gone
to leave we un-sober
probers alone
each in his gloomy pew
when we secretly desired
to ride wildly
along magic courses
of endless racetracks
within our emotional
quicksands.
Instead
we merely wonder
what worthless trophy
might await the one who
first arrives home.

The Lonely Elk Hotel

Marooned in a hunger
of blackberry loneliness
groggier than brandy
in feverish circles running forever.

Silence stalks the deserted corridors
in dead of night
to pause by doors
listen in keyhole silence
to clink of glass.
Insane winos
having lost the key to insight
drinking in the dark.
Harmonica players
recalling in silence
vain dreams.

Behind one door
redolent with scent
a brassy-haired woman
thrashing in sleep
a cynic about love
calls a name.

Other drunks
in isolated rooms
relay long snores
along dim passageways.
Occasional screams
raise dust devils
through this galaxy
of cubicles.

Midnight brain in break-neck canter
cradled in terror
in bare sleeping rooms
in a lonely city
on a lost street
inside the lonely Elk Hotel.

In Restless Sleep

Those birds
Those birds
That glide by night
On farther shores than here
Are resting on a cold black lake
And soon will re-appear.

Wet Season in San Francisco

There are days when nothing opens.
Front doors, back yards, wardrobes,
Keyholes, wallets, womens arms.
All afternoon I sat in the gloomy lobby
Watching the falling rain.

Thanksgiving

Drunk and hungry
my Thanksgiving dinner
disappeared down a whiskey glass.
Some chef's fabled giblet gravy
simmers forever
in a lost stock pot.
And home-baked pumpkin pie,
sliced for bearers of good tidings,
vanished somewhere between
a laugh suspended in space
and the tavern door.

Light Rain in Reno

Pop-eyed
he stared
as noisy boxcars
drifted in random chaos
down any swollen river
and
except to himself
the compulsive gambler
meaningless
as light rain.

The Mole

Small, fine-fingered mole.
Blind eyes
piercing non-light.
Tunneling forever
in the dark.
Toward the end
of your black journeys
what substitutes
for the great blinding flash
of the sun ?

Nature's Charms

For those who contemplate
the finer profiles of nature's charms;
the fallen leaf,
its skeletal spine,
cairn-studded cliffs
on wintry nights,
compelling in their stark beauty.
Despite abstract thought
on enchanted lakes
bearing golden swans,
keep in mind that birds still die
of gunshot wounds,
boys lose hands
on Sunday afternoons
in the woods
when chainsaw silence
cuts the air
with lack of sound,
and beside green tables
bankrupt gamblers
beg for credit,
and drunkards
through log-jammed throats
bay their torments
to the passing
disinterested clouds.

The Condor

I am the giant condor
Sailing above highways.
I wheel through sky
And tear at stars.
I assault space.
In my mournings
I hate as ice.

Yet my beak is green
My raiment black.
I have nine wives
who write my name
on the pages of earth.

Immobile above cloud
I am the lonely condor.
With red eyes
Disagreeable in life
my pulse thunders.
I survey jungles
to salve the savage within me.

The Lonely Carnival Horses

The lonely carnival horses
wooden - uncourted
anchored in sadness,
in some no-mans land of the mind
dream themselves free.
A great ghost stallion
shakes flaked paint from his shoulders
paces high ground
guards against intruders
rears high on hind feet,
snorts, stares, waits impatiently
as the ring of wooden mares
unwind from their circle
then down strange paths
break into fast running.

April Again

and the mad ram
barges
past other shambled Aprils
seeking new pastures.
Not, even now, clear
as to destinations.
Glares all about
seeking
tall pinnacles
to behead
in his drive
of life force.
Crosses hillsides
to beat down giants.
Fifty-eight years
devour the air
in mighty mouthfuls.
what is left ?
Best try
to conjure laughter
even under the coffin lid
a hundred years
or more
from now.

Banwell Hill   for Dick, my Brother

Over Banwell Hill,
hound-bayed, unbounded,
in memoried thought,
like a pulse-beat,
the nursery rhyme, Jack and Jill,
continues to wander
out of sight there,
and Dick, he sings still.
Deeper than time
in its dinosaur demise,
farther than tomorrow's awakening
or tonight's moonrise,
down sleeping avenues
where we struggle with our snores
he is lost no longer
as I here scatter his ashes
over this uncut moor.
I wonder why he lost an eye
and stayed home.
and I lost nothing
and stayed nowhere ?
His roistered time is come and gone
without personal message,
directing me in no direction
except to places
where I never seem to belong.

Driving Through a Scottish Village

the driver paused
to allow
seven goslings
resembling small scrubbed girls
in Sunday-best dresses
stepping as do geese
in single file
to cross to the other side
of this lost country road
and
for a moment
it seemed
that all the myths of Scotland
appeared
to pause and watch and wait
as we did
in this Stone Age village
beneath the shoulder
of a gaunt heathered hill
ancient as snow
with the earth arrested
in time up-ended;
then we drove on.

Walking the Dogs

in the railroad yard
the wind dries the high ridges
of the tracks
made by the yellow tractor
that moves rails
rusted to the brown colour
of a penny
and crossties so old
the creosote smell is gone.
Around the edges
of the drying mud puddles
the dog's footprints
make me think
of mammoth tracks in Siberia
and dinosaur bones.
I take a stick and with it sign my name
to register my presence to the wind.

A Consideration on the Possible Joys of Suicide

About to meet his maker
within his normal condition
of never-enoughness
the once barefoot boy
no longer in innocence resplendent
again by seascape dreaming
wades out.
This time too far
too deep
overanxious to meet the welcoming horizon
of green sea;
frolic with dolphins
bark with the ballad-singing walrus bulls
sidle into strange dances
with seal ladies
whose long green hair
entwines among the seaweed.
In rough and tumble seahorse canter
wave barnacled sea-wand
across the dark and dim-lit
sea bottom.
Harpstruck, star-struck, dumbstruck,
stumbling not heavenwards
yet happy in the knowing
that at last
his forever is come.

St. Patrick's Night

At a bar
drinking Schenley's
a green bird
flew
into the shipwrecked tavern.
Only I saw it.
The bird asked me the way
but I turned aside.
I too was lost.

Drinking and wishing for company
none came
and at closing time
I fought my way outside
through a tunnel
of cardboard shamrocks.

Horses and uniformed cops
long departed
and the bagpiper
walking lonely
from the lighted house.

Dirge of an Old Warrior

When I die
hang this shirt of fire
below an old shield
found in a field.
Hang it high in some hall
where suit of mail, dirk and spear,
needs no more this arm to wield.

Display these artifacts,
ornaments, souvenirs,
that historians trace,
curious tourists admire,
vandals deface;
that unarmed men who dare,
attempt to realize the peculiar problems
of turning sword into plowshare.

Reality and Dream

In a room scented of lavender
and stale bacon fat
he lives in solitude
heedless of neighbours
nor lets his mind dwell
long on affairs
of the immediate
or long range.

Let me jail-break out
from this cocoon of a room
claim a place in life
embrace strangers
with stars in their eyes
seek heritage with brothers.
A mad angel
I will emerge
to go stalking
the lost islands of wild imagination
the enchanted fields of peace.

Search

Sixty-two and still seeking my Father's attention.
The infectious smile I never knew
or true note of false praise.
No game playing to mellow the evenings,
nor even grimace of derision.
Were his embraces all exhausted
hauling barrels or hugging women ?
Never was I a compliment kissed.
Poverty rotted his soul.
Hardships hardened his arteries,
Drink drowned his kindness.
Frustration silenced his language.
To this day, in certain moods,
a ravage of tumult raging inside
attempts to claw its savage way free.
Drives me abroad
to walk expectant streets,
sure in my fury of knowing
that around the next corner
a man labouring,
some barker outside a store,
salesman having his shoes shined,
will be He.

After our eyes meet
we will hurry toward each other
to hug and love. And,
after regaining our composure
we will attempt to greet each other
for the first time.

Flying Scot, on hearing of his Father's Death

Desolate,
forever sailing
crewless phantom ship,
failing, for lack of breath
to cast off from abandoned carousels,
infested with spider webs.
Inevitable albatross about his neck,
seeking to guide drowned companions home.
Grey, fire-flied piles of desolate jetties drift by.
Muffled foghorns snore and bray.
Chartless, he feels,
to pilot fingertip way
from landlocked bay,
desiring freedom of the wide sea
but time takes its own good time.
Chill nights,
with seabirds grieving,
haunt his dreams.
Cold as Antarctica,
still as stone,
poignant as wailings
of a broken-hearted mermaid,
en route to Dunoon
where his Father lies dead.

Ode to Mistletoe

Suspended
over star-tipped top
of the glittering plastic Xmas tree
hung on a gas bracket
white-berried mistletoe
drapes and drifts
oddly out of kissable way
while merrily
from a faraway kitchen
the steam kettle whistles a Xmas carol.

Alone and dozing by base of ruby-red-wine keg
I listen closely
hear unknown whispers
perhaps Vespers ?
softly brittle flutterings
as of ancient bearded poets
pondering in taut voices
mystical observances
to make one wonder
in attempting more concentrated listen
do my ears actually bristle ?
or is it merely me, and wine, alone,
all sense flown,
lying alongside the wreckage of the cooked goose
burnt rum
blackberry brandy
listening intently
within a library of unspoken words
clearly hear whispers
nibbling under lath and plaster,
rustling mouse-whiskered tiptoe sounds
Xmas quiet as unbitten nut
gnawing to whittle the cross-grained floor away
under where I lie.

Shall I die here ?
fall through to a different land ?
Elsewhere in the house now
in runaway stride
broad roughshod voices bawl carols and ballads.
Shall I rise to add howling cry ?
rather hide
better to wait
celebrate beneath the floorboards
join the unseen feasting mice
in field and dormouse prance
toast one more well-cellared mousetime season
down there where other mistletoe
is hung for worship
on a different gas bracket ?

Or, deeper yet, let my heyday evening drowse
sink farther into doze of dream
till mellow walls of last unminding
lets memory flare farther
so that at last
merely by lying here
mistletoe in my hair
I am the last of the minstreled wanderers.
I am become the white berry of the mistletoe
worshipped since before Stonehenge.
Lovers beneath me kiss and love
Together we will depart to another place
where Xmas is more than berried mistletoe
and lasts forever.

Leonard Irving was born in the village of Dundrennan, in Scotland, a long time ago. His wild career includes service in the Royal Marines during World War II, and great distances travelled on ships, on trains and by simple walking. He presently resides in Oakland, CA, arguing with the sparrows outside his window each morning.

Elinor Randall was born in New England, twined in and out of horses, chickens and decayed farm machinery. She studied drawing with Marshall Glasier and George Grosz in New York City. She is a member of the Graphic Arts Workshop in San Francisco, where she puts lines and dots onto zinc plates.

Cover by Ken Ruffner
Cover Photo by E. Randall Keeney
Typeface Palatino
Printing by Precision Graphics

Stone Circle Press Institute of Celtic Studies
Oakland, California.